CW01091538

Snooker Basics: How to Play Snooker

ISBN-13: 978-1479143269

ISBN-10: 147914326X

Copyright Notice

SNOOKER BASICS: HOW TO PLAY SNOOKER

Steven Curid

I dedicate this book to every person – who has been lucky enough to have their lives touched by the joy, excitement and sheer buzz of snooker...

Contents

The History of Snooker

Snooker traces its history back to the nineteenth century, when British military officers used it as a way to pass the time at night.

It got its name from a member of the British Armed Forces who enjoyed calling the losing players a snooker, which is a term used to refer to first year cadets and inexperienced military personnel.

The name has stuck since then and this billiards game is still called by the same name even after all these years.

Sometime in the late 1800s, one of the officers decided to make a few variations to their game by adding differently-coloured balls to the usual red and black. This is why you now see different forms of the billiards game.

The sport grew so much in popularity that it continued to evolve from the time it was developed until the early twentieth century. The very first organized tournament, which was called the Amateur English Championships, was held in 1916. And in 1927, the world witnessed the very first Snooker World Championship.

This tournament was organized with the help of Joe Davis, a professional billiards player who wanted to transform snooker from simply a recreational activity for amateurs to a sport appreciated and participated in by professionals. Davis proceeded to win every single world championship from that time until he retired in 1946.

It was during the 1930s when snooker very quickly gained popularity and even became the most popular billiards game in many countries.

This popularity, however, saw a significant decline in the 1950s and early 1960s. Joe Davis even tried to reinvent snooker by introducing Snooker Plus, but that still didn't bring the sport back to its original popularity. It was in the late 1960s and early 1970s when the sport once again started gaining momentum as a result of televised snooker matches shown on BBC. The very first televised snooker tournament was called Pot Black and it was shown as part of the promotional campaign for colour TV.

In 1973, the world saw the Snooker World Championship on TV for the very first time.

This helped the sport gain even more popularity, as more people began watching and playing it. And in 1976, world rankings were introduced for the first time.

All these factors worked to bring snooker back into the mainstream as a number of new and talented players began to emerge. These young and dedicated players were the ones who turned snooker into the sport we know today. And though the sport has once again experienced ups and downs in its popularity over the next few years, it has continued to be one of the most watched games on TV to this day.

The history of snooker is indeed fascinating, especially for people who want to learn the sport. The more you read about the sport and its origins, the more you get to appreciate it and perhaps the more you'll want to play it.

What was once simply a form of recreation for the British Army has now become a sport that enchants people from across the globe.

The Popularity of Snooker

Just like darts, snooker has been a very popular and commonly-watched sport on British television ever since it's first airing in the early 1970s.

This was true even when many people were still trying to decipher what the coloured balls meant and how the game is played.

Even now, television ratings for snooker tournaments remain strong. Despite strong support, though, the sport is currently suffering from some sort of image problem. It has even been said that snooker is a dying sport. This is why the World Professional Billiards and Snooker Association is now actively seeking ways to solve this problem.

Sir Rodney Walker, chairman of the association, says they're now looking for imaginative ways of presenting the sport to the public.

Snooker is said to be a hundred times more difficult and challenging than pool, yet it still falls behind in terms of popularity.

The problem, according to older generation players, is that there are very few things that can be changed without completely changing the spirit of the sport.

Lately, however, a quicker-paced form of the game has been introduced and many are hoping this form will make the sport more appealing. The new form of snooker is called Super6, and it involves shorter matches and fewer balls.

Judging from what's happening in China so far, it looks like the prayers of snooker enthusiasts are indeed being heard. The sport has become so popular in the country that a first round match during the recent world championship successfully drew about a hundred million television viewers.

It has even gotten to the point that China offered to host the next Snooker World Championship. Walker, however, said that it's too soon to move the tournament outside of Britain and the association is also apprehensive about jeopardizing the strong support they're still getting from the BBC.

Even in Canada, snooker is experiencing an increase in interest and popularity. In fact, a new snooker academy has recently been opened to the public and it aims to teach young individuals new skills in the sport.

Canada will also be the host of this year's IBSF Under 21 World Championships, which should once again attract snooker enthusiasts from all over the world. There are even plans for a referee and coaching certification program to be developed in the country.

Finally, the country plans on hosting a number of amateur tournaments in the coming years, with the prize money being pegged at $25,000 to $50,000.

Within the next few years, very talented young players are expected to make their mark in international snooker tournaments and contribute to the popularity of the sport. And because of the recent decline in popularity, the recent developments of the sport in China and Canada could be nothing but good news, as it enables enthusiasts to look forward to a more global future for the sport.

If the surge of popularity in China continues, and if Canada's plans for more amateur tournaments pushes through, then the future is indeed bright for the sport of snooker.

Benefitting from
Snooker Lessons

Many people in different parts of the world are starting to become interested in learning how to play snooker.

The sport has indeed gained such popularity that a lot of individuals are now getting into the game, whether for recreation or competition purposes.

Snooker is indeed an excellent game to play for people who want to go out socialising and do more than just sit around a bar with a drink in hand.

Of course, the game is also popularly played as both an amateur and a professional sport. This would explain why snooker facilities are now found in all sorts of places worldwide.

The good news is that the rules of the game are pretty straightforward, thus making it easy for you to familiarise them. Take note, however, that you'll need more than just knowledge of the game rules in order to do well in this game.

This is particularly true if you plan to become good enough to compete in any of the existing snooker tournaments.

Just like any other sport, there are certain skills you'll have to master if you really want to become a successful snooker player.

Other than that, you'll also have to learn as much as you can about several different important factors such as stance, precision, and cue control.

You have to bear in mind that snooker is one game that requires a considerable amount of concentration and control. If you've never played any type of cue sport before, then learning the rules of snooker will definitely be the very least of your concerns.

It is for this reason that many people who want to learn snooker or who are already playing the game and want to improve their skills have decided to take advantage of snooker lessons.

These lessons typically cover a wide range of extremely important elements of the sport that'll help you learn more about the sport. The lessons also allow you to develop your skills in snooker or improve on the skills you already have, as they teach you about stance, taking aim, making the basic shots, basic play positions, and cut control, among other things.

If you've been playing snooker for some time purely for purposes of recreation and now want to take your skills to a competitive level, then there are also a lot of benefits for you to gain from snooker lessons.

In your case, advanced snooker lessons may be advisable, since you're already familiar with the basics of the game. This type of lessons typically covers a range of snooker skills on more advanced levels.

It'll likely include taking advanced shots, playing advanced positions, and safety and defense. You'll be surprised at how much you can learn and how quickly you'll be able to master the game with the help of snooker lessons.

But, perhaps the best thing about these lessons is the fact that they're now available in online versions, which means you can easily learn the ins and outs of the sport without having to leave the comfort of your home.

Rules of Snooker

If you're serious about learning to play snooker, then it's definitely important for you to know the game rules.

While this may actually be the least of your problems, it's a necessary first step towards learning the sport.

Perhaps the first thing you need to know is the object of the game, which is to score more points than your opponent. Pretty simple and straightforward, right? Yes, but achieving that objective is definitely a lot more challenging than it seems.

Each ball in snooker has a specific point value. The red balls, of which there can be three, six, ten, or fifteen in a game, have a point value of one.

Yellow balls have a point value of 2, green balls three, brown balls 4, blue balls 5, pink balls 6, and black balls 7. One ball of each colour is used in every snooker game. Then, of course, you have the white-coloured cue ball, which has no value at all. Points are scored either by legally potting the red or coloured balls, or when your opponent commits a foul.

In snooker, the first player who breaks is randomly chosen. He is required to position the cue ball within the Half Circle and then cause it to make contact with a red ball; otherwise, a foul is committed.

A foul in this case gives the other player the option of either accepting the table and moving to strike or requiring his opponent to be the striker. Each time a ball is potted legally, the striker's turn at the table shall continue until he either wins the frame or fails to pot a ball.

As soon as the first red ball is potted, the next objective would be to pot a coloured ball. And for as long as there are red balls on the table, a play should keep alternating between reds and colors.

If the object of play is currently a coloured ball, the striker must designate a specific color ball as the object of his play. The cue ball should then make contact first with that ball before it hits any other balls. Failure to do so is a foul. When there aren't any reds left on the table, the object of play becomes the coloured balls in ascending order based on their point value.

Fouls are called whenever you fail to make contact with a red ball on the break shot and when you fail to make contact with the object ball first. A foul is also committed when you pot a color ball during a play where your object ball is red and vice versa. You also commit a foul when the cue ball enters a pocket and if you pot any other ball when your object is a specific color ball.

Whenever you commit a foul, your opponent will be awarded a minimum of four points and a maximum of seven.

The awarded point is typically the higher value between the value of the object ball and the value of the ball that was hit instead. A snooker game ends when every single ball has been potted.

A Quick Look at
Snooker Tables

In the world of billiards, the full-sized snooker table is considered as the biggest beast, along with the Russian pyramid table. It measures 12 feet in length and 6 feet in width, so you'll definitely need a considerable amount of space to place it in if you ever decide to buy one for yourself.

Many snooker enthusiasts do, indeed, buy their own snooker table for the simple reason that it can be a joy to own. The table has a total of six pockets, composed of four corner pockets and two middle pockets. It can indeed be quite an imposing piece of furniture.

The snooker table and its side cushions are covered in woollen cloth that features a nap, which is a special set of raised fibres that makes the cloth feel furry.

The nap has a specific direction on the table from the baulk right to the black spot end. It is rough towards the baulk end and smooth towards the black spot end.

This allows the cue ball to deviate a bit, particularly when it runs slowly against the nap and serves as an added hazard in a snooker game.

The table requires ironing after a few games in order to restore the nap's direction on the woollen cloth.

The snooker table itself is made of wood, usually either mahogany or golden oak, and is characterised by a slate playing surface. The table's frame can substantially carry the weight of the slate, which typically comes in four or five pieces for easy transport.

Depending on the table manufacturer, the pieces of slate can be anywhere from ¾ to 1 ½ inches thick. When put together, a snooker table generally weighs about a ton, which is why it typically has eight legs.

The good news is that you can place the table on normal floorboards without any problem, since its weight is evenly spread out among its eight legs.

Take note, though, that there are a number of subtle differences between snooker tables used at home and those that are used in tournaments. Competition tables typically have tighter pockets, which make the balls a bit more difficult to pot.

The cloth on these tables is also changed more often to provide the players with consistent results.

Professional players naturally know how the balls should respond on the snooker table and even the subtlest differences matter a lot to these players, which is why you'll often hear them complain about a cloth that's slightly worn or isn't properly ironed. This is especially true when there's big prize money involved.

The cushions in snooker tournaments are also different because they're backed with steel to make sure the bounce remains the same.

This theory is premised on the fact that the cushion rubber isn't glued onto a piece of wood, which can alter the ball's rebound slightly. Just as with the cloth, only professional players are likely to notice the difference.

Of course, if you plan to purchase your own snooker table, you first need to make sure you have enough space to position the table properly and to move around during a game. You should also make sure the room you place it in isn't damp, as that can have a negative effect on the wood and cloth.

Choosing a Snooker Cue

If you seriously want to become a good snooker player, then you'd do well to consider buying your own snooker cue.

Choosing the right snooker cue can be a daunting task for those who are new to the game, so you may want to check out the following tips on what to look for in a snooker cue.

Take note that there are generally four main differences between the various cue brands and styles.

These differences are the weight, length, wood type, and types of split.

These are perhaps your most important considerations when you start shopping for a new snooker cue.

When you consider the weight of a snooker cue, your choice is basically a matter of feel. There isn't a specific weight suggested to improve your snooker skills. What you need to do is find a cue with just enough weight to allow you to make a clean break.

Bear in mind that heavier cues enable you to break with more force than you'd have with a lighter cue.

Heavier cues can help you hide a poor shot whereas lighter cues can give more spin to the cue ball. The drawback to heavier cues is that they tend to tire out an inexperienced player a lot more quickly. You may want to take this fact into serious consideration.

Snooker cues are generally about 58 inches long. Of course, the length of a cue may vary according to the model type. Take note that longer cues provide you with more reach, but it can also be a bit heavier. You'd want to take these attributes into consideration when choosing the right length for your snooker cue.

Just like with the weight, there's no specific cue length that's recommended for snooker players. Your choice will depend largely on your preference as regards how a particular cue feels when you use it.

It would therefore be wise to try using cues of different weights and lengths first before going out to buy one for yourself.

Most snooker cues are made from either Maple or Ash. Ash is generally considered stiffer than Maple and its wood has a highly visible grain whereas the grain of Maple is extremely tight.

Again, the choice of wood type is largely a matter of feel and one isn't necessarily better than the other. These days, however, you're likely to find considerably more cues made from Ash as Maple cues have somehow become fewer in number.

Modern cues currently being used by younger players are made of fibreglass or carbon fibre. You may also want to try handling cues made from different materials to see which one works best for you.

As regards the types of split, one-piece cues are often the traditional choice of snooker players. Not only do they look brilliant, but they also give you a smoother feathering action.

The drawback is that their length and lack of a joint can make them a bit difficult to carry around. The two-piece cue, as its name suggests, can be split into two equal parts.

This is perhaps the most popular type of cue at present because it can easily be carried around and doesn't take up too much space. The drawback there's a seam that can interrupt the feathering action.

Keener snooker players usually choose the three-quarter jointed cue, which break up about eight inches from the base on both ends, thus giving you no problems with feathering.

Choosing the right cue can definitely increase your chances of becoming a successful snooker player.

Snooker Techniques

Snooker is a two-player billiards game that's becoming increasingly popular in different parts of the world.

Simply put, you strike the cue ball with a cue stick and earn scores by hitting the object balls into the pockets. If you want to be good in this sport, then you'll have to develop excellent eye-hand coordination.

Furthermore, you'll also need to develop your bridging hand, a strong grip, a good stance, smooth shooting, and such techniques as cue ball spinning.

Here's how you can develop stronger snooker skills:

1. Bridging

Form a bridge with your hand that's not holding the cue stick. This is done by making a "V" shape with your thumb and index finger. Place this hand palm-down right in front of the cue ball and then position your cue stick on the bottom tip of the V.

Adjust your bridging hand in such a way that the tip of your cue stick is sure to hit the cue ball at just the right place. The distance of your bridge from the cue ball will depend largely on the amount of backswing you want to apply. This will, in turn, depend largely on the amount of force you want to hit the cue ball with.

2. Gripping

Wrap the forefinger and thumb of your shooting hand firmly around the bottom part of your cue stick. Be careful, though, not to hold the stick so tight that it prevents you from moving fluidly. As soon as you execute the backswing, you have to make sure your other fingers are kept away from the cue stick until you're done shooting. This helps ensure smooth stick movement.

3. Stance

You need to stay completely still as you make your shot. Your shooting arm should be the only part of your body that moves. In order to achieve this, you'll have to execute a firm stance. If you normally shoot with your right hand, then you'd do well to point your right foot in the same direction as your intended shot.

Keep your right leg straight and your left leg comfortably bent. Make sure your chest and chin are positioned as close to the cue ball as possible as you make your shot.

4. Shooting

As soon as you've formed and positioned your bridge, angle your cue stick such that it is perfectly aligned in the general direction of the shot you plan to make. Practice moving your cue backward and forward before you actually strike the cue ball.

Before taking the shot, be sure to take a look at the cue ball, your object ball, and the pocket where you plan to sink the object ball. When you're ready to make the shot, pull your cue backward along the bridge, pause briefly, and then strike the cue ball smoothly.

5. Ball Spinning

Spins can make the cue ball slide, curve, or jump. If you want to achieve a slide, then you need to strike the cue ball just below its centre point.

To make a right curve, you'll have to strike the cue ball towards the left of its centre point and vice versa to make a left curve.

If you want to make the cue ball jump over another ball in order to successfully hit your object ball, then you'll have to strike it well below the centre point. You may also put a backspin on the cue ball by hitting it a little below centre point.

Learning Snooker:
Three Basic Skills

If you truly want to become a good snooker player, then you'll have to master three basic snooker skills.

Cue Ball Control

The importance of this skill lies in the fact that the game of snooker doesn't just require you to focus on potting balls and then hoping the cue ball will stop at the perfect spot for you to make the next shot. You'll have to plan your shots ahead and learn how to accurately read the game.

A good snooker player is someone who can play a stop shot, a draw-back, and a follow-on shot at the appropriate time. A stop shot is the kind of shot where the cue ball stops almost immediately after hitting the object ball. This can be an excellent way of positioning the cue ball, since it lets you know almost exactly where it will stop.

To achieve this shot, you'll have to strike the cue ball in the centre. This can, however, vary according to the distance of your object ball from the cue ball.

A draw-back is executed to make the cue ball roll backwards after it hits the object ball. This shot is achieved by striking the cue ball below the centre point. As a general rule, the lower you strike the cue ball, the more it will roll back.

Another way to make the ball roll back farther is to hit it with more power. For its part, a follow-on shot is typically used to make the cue ball roll farther forward after it hits the object ball. The shot is achieved by hitting the cue ball above its centre point.

In contrast to the draw-back, the general rule for this shot is that the higher you hit the cue ball, the farther forward it will roll.

Take note that playing these two shots increases the risk of miscuing your shot, thus making it very important to practice them repeatedly before you even attempt to use them in a high-stakes competition.

Potting Skills

There is perhaps no need to explain why your ability to pot balls is vital to becoming a good snooker player.

In order to pot the right balls, you'll have to learn about the right angles at which you'd want your object ball to travel and then strike the area directly opposite the object ball with your cue ball.

This may sound easy in theory, but when you try putting it into practice you'll realise that it's a lot more difficult than it sounds.

You need to consider at all times the amount of power you need to hit the cue ball with, especially since using too much power can make your object ball bounce right out of the pocket.

On the other hand, too little power can result in the object ball failing to reach the pocket.

Safety Skills

Every snooker player uses a safety shot from time to time. In fact, the very first shot played in a game is usually a safety shot. This is basically a shot that leaves your opponent without a clear shot at the object ball.

It is typically played when the chances of potting the object ball is very slim. This is because missing a pot in a snooker match usually causes the player to lose the game.

Excellent cue ball control and good potting skills may make you a confident snooker player, but you'll only be truly on your way to success when you learn to play the safety shots well.

Why Stance is Important

If you've already started playing snooker, then you'll likely to be already aware that there are a few things you may have to do in order to improve your game. among these things are developing cue control, improving your positioning, and even making sure the equipment you use are all of good quality.

You need to take note as well that your stance is a key aspect to playing good snooker.

To put it simply, stance refers to the way you're positioned at the snooker table as you take your shots.

You may not realise it, but stance is actually one of the most important aspects of becoming a good snooker player.

This is why you need to develop a good snooker stance and be consistent in executing that stance in every one of your games if you truly want to be a consistently good snooker player.

Now, you may be wondering just what it is that makes the stance very important in improving your snooker game.

Well, there are several reasons why stance is considered as one of the keys to a good snooker game and those reasons include the following:

1. Balance

Needless to say, your stance can greatly affect your balance as you take a shot in snooker. In order to make sure that your shot is smooth and accurate, you need to ensure that you're properly balanced, and that's one thing you can only truly achieve when you've developed a good stance.

2. Stability

As soon as you've mastered your snooker stance you'll realise that it gives you the kind of stability that allows you to take a much smoother and well-controlled shot when you try to pot the object balls.

A good snooker stance enables you to stand solidly and stay absolutely still as you take your shots, which is vital to ensuring the success of each shot you take.

3. Consistency

When you've mastered your snooker stance, one can safely say that you'll be able to position yourself correctly every time you take a shot.

As a result, every single shot you take should be as smooth and well-controlled as the last.

Consequently, this should translate into a much more consistent and ultimately better game.

Developing a good snooker stance also affects other areas of your game in a positive way. These areas include your grip, accuracy level, cue control, and your confidence level. Take note that the task of mastering a good snooker stance naturally comes more easily to some people than it does to others.

If you happen to be one of those people for whom the stance doesn't come so easily, then don't panic.

Just as with almost everything else in life, practice makes perfect. So, keep practicing your snooker stance until you get it right. When you do, keep practicing until you master it and it becomes second nature to you.

Soon you'll surely become so good at the sport you may even forget you had problems with your stance to begin with.

Holding Your Cue

Snooker is just one of the billiards games that many people enjoy playing. If you want to play the sport for competition purposes, then you'll have to master a number of different skills, including your stance and your aim.

Other than that, you'll also need to learn how to hold your snooker cue properly when you take your shots in a snooker game. Believe it or not, there are many people who start out playing this game without any idea on how to correctly hold the cue.

These people tend to approach the snooker table brandishing their cue without giving any thought at all to the proper holding style.

Take note, though, that the manner in which you hold your snooker cue can have a huge impact on how successful you are in the sport, especially where your aim is concerned.

The manner in which you hold your cue affects both the accuracy of your aim and the amount of power behind your shot. Of course, you can't really be expected to hold the cue correctly the very first time you step up to the table for a game of snooker.

However, that doesn't mean you shouldn't learn. In fact, you probably need to practise a number of times before you finally achieve the proper positioning of your hands on your cue.

Once you've learned how to hold the cue correctly and mastered it, you'll surely be able to tell the difference immediately, especially in terms of the power and control you're able to place behind every single shot you take.

You may want to bear in mind some general rules about holding your cue. To start with, holding the cue towards its lower end allows you to put more power behind your shots. However, doing this also sacrifices your aim.

In contrast, holding the cue too high up will allow for a much better aim, but will most probably deliver much less power behind your shots. The best thing for you to do is to hold the cue about a third of the way up. This allows you to maximise both your power and aim, which are both essential to the successful execution of a snooker shot.

Another thing you need to remember is that your index and middle fingers have to be positioned at the bottom of your cue, and your cue should rest comfortably between these fingers.

Make sure you don't grip the cue too tightly, as this will be a hindrance to making a smooth shot. You should try instead to aim for a much more relaxed hold on your cue, as this will help ensure that you can take a well-controlled and perfectly smooth shot.

Just like many of the other skills you need to develop for the sport of snooker, you'll soon realise that learning to hold your cue properly and comfortably will require a considerable amount of practice.

But, you can take assurance from the thought that once you master this skill, you'll be able to enjoy the game even more and achieve far greater success in the sport.

How to Break

Points may be earned both for offensive and defensive play, which is why safety play is typically encouraged.

Learning how to break well is a safety technique in itself.

Here's how you can shoot a safe break in snooker:

1. Take note that snooker balls roll differently on every snooker table.

   Among the factors that affect the way the balls roll are the type and age of the felt used, the levelness of the surface, and the level of humidity at the time of play. It's advisable for you to check the table's speed before a game starts by lagging your cue ball up and down the surface.

   You may also want to hit the cue ball hard enough to make it bounce off the foot bumper and then come to a stop as close as possible to the head bumper. Observe how it feels when you hit the cue ball at that speed and then base your other shots on that observation.

2. It doesn't really matter which side of the rack you break, so it's best for you to choose the side you feel most comfortable shooting from.

   Practice breaking from that side and break from the same side each time you start a new game. Take note that the breaking player is allowed to take the cue ball in hand and position it anywhere within the half circle and behind the head string. You'd do well to place your cue ball such that you can easily hit the red ball in the back corner.

3. As mentioned earlier, you need to aim for the back corner red ball. Try to hit it as directly as you can without hitting the ball right in front of it.

4. Make sure you strike the cue ball just hard enough to hit the corner red ball thinly. The cue ball should then hit the bottom rail and then return to the head of the table.

5. This is what makes it important for you to have an idea of the table speed prior to the game. If you can't accomplish this, at least leave one tough shot for your opponent without any breakout possibilities.

6. The best results of a break leave your opponent without a shot on any of the red balls. Remember that you can score points from a bad hit from your opponent. The second best result mentioned earlier not only leaves your opponent without a breakout opportunity, but also without a safety opportunity.

If you're new to the sport, you may think the safety break described above will result in an incredibly long game, but you'll soon realise that it's a lot easier to beat your opponent by playing a smarter game.

Controlling the Cue Ball

In learning how to play snooker, one of the most important things you need to bear in mind is that the most important ball on the table is the white-coloured cue ball.

After all, this is the only ball you strike directly with your cue. For this reason, your ability to control the cue ball is vital to improving your snooker skills.

Remember as well that controlling the cue ball isn't all about being able to pot the other balls. It also involves planning ahead as well as accurately maneuvering the cue ball.

Screw and Stun

This is the most commonly-used spin in snooker. You can achieve it by hitting the lower half of your cue ball. If you hit just below the centre of the cue ball, then you can successfully stop it dead.

But, if you want to give it more of a backspin, then you need to hit it a bit lower. You have to be careful not to hit the cue ball too low, as that can cause it to jump. If you really overdo it, then you may even end up ripping the cloth covering of the snooker table.

Where direction is concerned, you can screw back in a perfectly straight line by striking the bottom centre of the cue ball. If you want to send the ball right or left, then you need to strike its lower sides.

Top Spin

When you strike the upper part of the cue ball, it is likely to travel farther after it hits the object ball.

You'd do well to raise your bridge hand when you execute this particular shot. Doing so helps steady your aim and allows for greater accuracy when you strike the top centre of the cue ball. This shot is frequently used by snooker players who want to open a pack or red balls.

You should also concentrate on the follow-through you make with your cue after you strike the cue ball.

Take note that it is a good combination of power, the distance between the cue ball and the object ball, and the follow-through that determines how much spin you successfully place on the cue ball.

Side Spin

This is probably the most difficult technique to successfully use. In fact, even professional snooker players typically have some difficulty judging and executing the side spin.

This technique is used for a number of different reasons, but its primary purpose is to change the angle at which the cue ball bounces off of the cushion after it hits the object ball.

The side spin is achieved by striking either the centre left or centre right of the cue ball. Imagine that you just hit the cue ball with a left side spin. It's likely to bounce off of the cushion farther to the left after it hits the object ball.

The same is true with the right side spin. Once you're able to perfect this skill, you can also start using it to swerve the cue ball, which is sometimes required for you to avoid being snookered.

Improving Your Cue Action

Solid cue action in snooker naturally stems from confidence. This means you shouldn't dwell on negative thoughts about your abilities and the game itself because that'll only cause you to lose your concentration and may ultimately cost you the game.

When you start thinking negatively about your snooker skills, the best thing for you to do may be to get back to the basics and try to develop a pre-shot routine.

Here are some tips on how to solve your confidence problems and consequently improve your cue action in snooker:

1. Observe Others in Action

Look at how the best snooker players go about their game and you'll realise they share one thing in common: They all keep absolutely still when they take a shot.

Remember that these players were once where you are right now and they were able to improve their technique through a lot of practice. You need to bear in mind, therefore, that it's important to improve your concentration and stillness when playing snooker.

Ironically, your stillness can best be improved by developing your concentration and your concentration can best be developed by giving your brain something to focus on. And what better to focus on than taking your shots, right?

2. Keep Still and Choose Your Shot

The first thing you need to do as part of your mental pre-shot routine is to decide on the shot you want to take.

As you make this decision, you should also decide on how much power you want to apply and what type of positioning you want to achieve for the next ball. In essence, you need to program your brain by imagining yourself actually taking the shot in your mind. Once you've gone through this mental exercise, you should be more confident in taking your position at the snooker table and preparing to take the actual shot.

3. Check Your Stance

Never forget the basics of a good snooker stance. Your lead foot should point down the line of your intended shot and your other leg should be bent comfortably.

Make sure your stance is solid enough to assure you of a smooth shot. You may want to lean into the table a bit.

It's also advisable for you to designate two specific points down the cue line that'll serve as your sight in the same way you would look through the sight of a gun. This effectively strengthens the mental programming you started in your pre-shot routine.

4. Take the Shot

Take note that this is typically where everything goes drastically wrong, so you need to be very careful in taking the actual shot. This is when you're most in need of confidence. So, tell yourself that you're sure of what shot to take and you know you have a good stance.

Now, concentrate on striking the cue ball right on the point you intended to hit and don't forget to follow through so you'll see exactly where the cue ball travelled. As much as possible, you should maintain your shot position until the balls have all come to rest and you've (hopefully) achieved what you wanted with the shot.

Three Tips for Improving Your Snooker Game

So, you already know how to play snooker. In fact, you may be playing it almost regularly as a way to pass the time or enjoy some bonding time with family and friends.

Now, what if you want to take your snooker game to the next level and join a few amateur competitions?

What if you're actually looking forward to going pro at some point in the future?

How can you enhance your skills and improve your overall game?

Here are three useful tips you may want to take note of in your journey towards becoming a successful snooker player:

1. Keep the Basics in Mind

The most basic skill in playing snooker is your stance and you shouldn't take this for granted even as you advance in the sport. You should always keep your legs about a shoulder width apart and remember to always keep your back straight as well.

Looking straight down your cue is also extremely important when you take a shot because this enables you to see the direction of the ball after you've made your shot. Always make sure your cue action is smooth and steady, and never try to execute complicated shots unless you're already confident that you've mastered the basics of the sport.

2. Vary Your Competition

As mentioned above, you may enjoy an occasional game of snooker with family and friends. But, if you want to go pro and truly want to bring your snooker game to the next level, then you'll have to take on better competition as well.

Playing with a better snooker player challenges you to raise your game a notch. Of course, this doesn't mean you have to play with better players all the time.

In fact, that may be counter-productive, as it can take much of your confidence away when you lose every game you play.

What you need to do is vary your competition such that you win some games while also losing some. This should let you know what improvements you need to make.

3. Play Regularly

You've probably heard this too many times, but practice does make perfect, even in snooker. In order to improve your game, you'll have to play regularly. It's even advisable to play every day if you have the time.

You may want to consider buying a snooker table so you can practice every day with or without competition. Be careful not to play for too long, though, as that can lead to boredom and a poor game.

Naturally, having a poor game can lead to frustration and defeat any progress you may have made. What you need to do instead is to play shorter and more frequent snooker sessions with opponents of different skill levels.

There are, of course, several other tips that can help enhance your skills and take your snooker game to the next level, but these three basic rules should point you in the right direction.

If nothing else, it should assure you of having far more consistent snooker skills.

Practice

If you want to make your mark in the world of snooker, you will need to play a lot. Just like in any other sport, practise is the key to achieving an excellent snooker game and a majority of those who play in snooker tournaments typically spend hours each day just going through their routines and honing their skills.

Take note that when we talk about snooker practise, were not really talking about playing a few rounds with family and friends unless, of course, your family and friends are all professional snooker players as well.

If you're determined to become an excellent snooker player, then you'll have to spend some time practising your routines on your own. This is usually the time when you can focus and work on the different aspects of your game.

In fact, many of the competitive snooker players spend a few hours each day just practising alone and fine tuning their individual snooker skills.

Among the most important things for you to work on when you go through your practise routine are your stance, table positioning, alignment, cue action, cue control, and potting skills.

As your skills grow more advanced, you may also want to go through some of the more in-depth exercises and practise routines done by professional snooker players to assure themselves of a well-polished game.

If you've enhanced your snooker skills enough to finally go pro, then you'd do well to bear in mind that most professionals go through their practise routines as if they're playing an actual snooker match.

This means they don't allow anything to distract them while they're practising in the same way you won't let anything distract you when you're playing in an actual match.

Even if you're not yet good enough to go pro, but going pro is one of your goals, then you'd do well to practise the way a professional would.

However, if you simply want to improve your snooker skills so you don't always lose to your friends and you really don't have any plans of going pro, then you probably don't need to commit that much time to hard core practise the way professionals do.

Other ways to improve your skills include online videos and tutorials and DVDs that can teach you some exercises and practise routines. At the same time, these tools provide you with some helpful tips on improving the most important skills you need.

The good news is that there are now plenty of tools you can use for purposes of improving your snooker game and helping you enjoy the sport for years to come.

Printed in Poland
by Amazon Fulfillment
Poland Sp. z o.o., Wrocław